THE SAHARA DESERT
THE BIGGEST DESERT

Aileen Weintraub

The Rosen Publishing Group's
PowerKids Press™
New York

Published in 2001 by The Rosen Publishing Group, Inc.
29 East 21st Street, New York, NY 10010

First Edition

Book Design: Michael J. Caroleo
Illustration on page 15 by Michael J. Caroleo

Photo Credits: Cover image © Tiziana and Gianni Baldizzone/CORBIS; Title page/all backgrounds and pp. 4, 11 © CORBIS; p. 7 © FPG; p. 8 © Index Stock; p. 12 (both images) © George Holton/Photo Researchers Inc.; p. 15 (desert and figures) © Craig Aurness/CORBIS; p. 16 © Peter Arnold Inc.; p. 19 © Adam Woolfitt/CORBIS.; p. 20 © Travelpix 1997/ FPG.

Weintraub, Aileen, 1973-.
    The Sahara desert : the biggest desert / Aileen Weintraub.
        p. cm.— (Great record breakers in nature)
    Includes index.
    Summary: This book describes the different landforms and the recorded temperatures of the Sahara Desert, which is located on the continent of Africa.
    ISBN 0-8239-5640-7
    1.Sahara—Juvenile literature. [1. Sahara.] I. Title. II. Series.

DT334.W45 2000
966—dc21   00-039164

Manufactured in the United States of America

CONTENTS

4

A FAMOUS DESERT

Imagine a place on Earth that gets so hot you cannot live without water for more than four hours. Imagine walking in this place for hundreds of miles (km) and seeing only sand. This is the Sahara Desert, the largest desert in the world. The Sahara is located on the **continent** of Africa. It is 3.32 million square miles (8.6 million sq km). The desert runs through 11 countries and a part of Africa known as Western Sahara.

The Sahara stretches from the Atlantic Ocean in the west to the Red Sea in the east. It reaches more than 1,200 miles (1,931 km) from the Atlas Mountains and Mediterranean Sea in the north to the Sahel **region** in the south.

◀ *The Sahara Desert is so big, it is practically the same size as the United States.*

A CHANGE IN TEMPERATURE

The word "Sahara" means "desert" in the Arabic language. An eastern part of the Sahara is known as the Eastern or Arabian Desert. An area known as the Libyan Desert is near the large North African country of Libya. The Sahara is one of the hottest places on Earth. The highest temperature in the world was recorded in the part of the Sahara that runs through Libya. One hot September day in 1922, the temperature in the Sahara soared to 136 degrees Fahrenheit (58 degrees C). Would you believe that the Sahara can be so hot during the day, but the temperature can drop down to below freezing at night? A winter's night in the Sahara can be very cold.

Temperatures in the Sahara can be extremely high during the day, and then drop to below freezing at night. ▶

ERGS, REGS, AND HAMMADAS

The Sahara Desert has many different landforms. Parts of the Sahara have sand **dunes**. A sand dune is a mountain of sand. Some dunes can be as high as 600 feet (183 m). These dunes are found in huge areas of shifting sand called **ergs**. **Regs** are another type of landform found in the desert. Regs are broad plains covered with sand and gravel. Regs make up most of the Sahara. **Hammadas** also make up a large part of the Sahara. Hammadas are areas of flat, raised land that are also known as **plateaus**. There are volcanic mountains in the Sahara in the country of Chad. Emi Koussi, a peak in the Tibesti Mountains is 11,204 feet (3,415 m) high. It is the highest point in the desert.

◄ *These towering sand dunes appear in the North African country of Morocco.*

IN SEARCH OF WATER

The sun shines strong all year round in the Sahara. Everybody loves sunshine, but what happens when there is almost no rain at all? The rainfall in the Sahara is usually less than 10 inches (25 cm) a year. In some parts of the Sahara, there is almost no rainfall for years. People cannot survive without water. There are very few lakes in the Sahara. Most of these lakes are saltwater lakes. This means that people cannot drink from them. Lake Chad is the only freshwater lake in the desert. Rivers once ran through the Sahara. We know this because dried-up riverbeds, called **wadis**, still exist. When it does rain in the desert, these wadis fill up with water and become active rivers for a short time.

This is a view of Lake Chad from the sky. Lake Chad is the only freshwater lake in the Sahara.

BEFORE THE DESERT

The Sahara is often called El Khela, meaning "the emptiness." It appears as though there is nothing but sand as far as the eye can see. This was not always the case. Thousands of years ago the Sahara was a region filled with animals, plants, and vegetables. We know this because scientists have found fossils and bones of crocodiles, hippopotamuses, elephants, and other animals. Scientists have also found large rocks covered with paintings. Ancient people who lived in the Sahara carved and painted pictures of what their lives were like. The scenes include drawings of cattle, hunters, and fishermen. Sometimes seashells can even be found in the Sahara. This proves that there was once a lot of water in this region.

◄ *The top drawing, done by ancient people to show their image of a god, was found in the country of Algiers. The bottom drawing of a giraffe and hunters was also done by early people.*

HOW THE SAHARA BECAME A DESERT

The Sahara Desert didn't form overnight. Thousands of years ago, the crust beneath the surface of Earth began to move. Some of Earth's **plates** began either to crash into one another or to pull apart. High mountains in the region of the Sahara began to crumble. Huge rocks were crushed into tiny grains of sand. Flowing rivers slowly dried up and disappeared. The winds changed direction. This made the desert hotter and drier. There was no water and the animals started dying. It became almost impossible for people to grow or find food. Most of the people living there had to leave. The closest **source** of water became the Nile River. The people of the Sahara moved east toward the Nile.

The outline map of Africa shows the location of the Nile River.

SAHARA DESERT

NILE
RIVER

ATLANTIC
OCEAN

WHO LIVES IN THE DESERT?

Even though the Sahara is the world's biggest desert, it has one of the lowest **population densities**. The entire desert has a population of only two and a half million people. That's fewer people than there are living in most large cities. Most of the people who live in the desert speak Arabic. The major religion in the Sahara is **Islam**. Small groups of Jewish and Christian people also live there.

Many people living in the Sahara are **nomads**. These people wander around from place to place looking for food and water. They don't settle anywhere for a very long time. People who do settle in the Sahara live on an **oasis**. An oasis is fertile land found near fresh water.

◀ *Oases, which are surrounded by desert like this one in Libya, have fresh water and fertile land for growing crops.*

AN OASIS IN THE DESERT

There are many rivers outside the Sahara. Water from these rivers enters the desert through underground **channels**. When this water rises to the surface of the desert, an oasis is formed. A village or small city can be built around an oasis. The Sahara has about 90 large oases and many small oases. People who live on these oases form a community. They survive by growing crops like dates, barley, and wheat. They also raise animals like sheep, goats, and cattle. The largest oases have fewer than 2,000 people. Some oases have as few as one or two families. They have green farmlands that are watered from wells that are over 1,000 feet (305 m) deep.

This is a market in an oasis. After traveling for days in the hot, barren Sahara, it is a pleasure to come across an oasis.

SURVIVING THE SAHARA

During the summer months, nomads tend to move to plateaus and mountains at the northern and southern ends of the Sahara. These areas are cooler. The people living in the Sahara wear clothes that are made of a thin, cool material. It is part of the **Muslim** tradition for men to cover their heads and wear baggy pants. Women wear veils and cover themselves from head to toe. At one time, camels were the main source of transportation. People from the Middle East first brought camels to the desert during the third century. Camel **caravans** carried goods to trade with people in other cities. Today, specially-equipped motortrucks and airplanes are used to cross the desert.

◄ *Camel caravans, like this one in the country of Tunisia, were used to trade a variety of goods, including salt, cloth, and gold.*

FAST FACTS ABOUT THE SAHARA

- ◆Sandstorms are very common in the desert. Brown clouds of sand cover the sky as wind blows sand everywhere.
- ◆Sometimes you can find gazelles and antelope in the sand dunes of the Sahara. Mostly, though, you will find birds, snakes, lizards, gerbils, and small foxes in the dunes.
- ◆Many desert animals search for food at night, when it is cooler.
- ◆People have said they can hear the desert sing. Nobody knows for sure how this happens, but if you ever find yourself in the Sahara, listen carefully. You might hear it, too.

GLOSSARY

caravans (KAYR-uh-vanz) Groups of travelers, carrying supplies and equipment, traveling in a line.

channels (CHAN-lz) The beds of streams or rivers, sometimes underground.

continent (KON-tin-ent) One of the seven great masses of land on Earth.

dunes (DOONZ) Mountains of sand.

ergs (ERGZ) Types of sand dunes found in the Sahara.

hammadas (hah-MAH-das) Flat, elevated land found in the Sahara.

Islam (IS-lam) A type of religion practiced by Muslims.

Muslim (MUHZ-lim) A person who believes in the Islamic religion.

nomads (NOH-madz) People who move from place to place with no single home.

oasis (oh-AY-sis) An area in a desert, near water, where people can live and raise crops.

plateaus (plah-TOHZ) Large areas of raised, flat land, known as hammadas in the Sahara.

plates (PLAYTS) The moving pieces of Earth's crust.

population densities (pop-yoo-LAY-shun DEN-sih-teez) The average numbers of people living in certain areas.

region (REE-jen) A large part of the earth's surface.

regs (REGZ) Broad, gravel-covered plains found in the Sahara.

source (SORS) The place where something starts.

wadis (WAH-dees) Dried-up riverbeds found in the desert.

INDEX

WEB SITES

To learn more about the Sahara Desert, check out these Web sites:
http://www.cia.gov/cia/publications/factbook/geos/wi.html
http://www.ontheline.org.uk/explore/nature/deserts/sahara.htm